Wilhelm Bender

WITH RAUPENSCHLEPPER OST ON THE EASTERN FRONT

Orel-Brjansk-Kowel-Warsaw-Danzig

TABLE OF CONTENTS

Published by PeKo Publishing Kft. · 8360 Keszthely, Bessenyei György utca 37., Hungary

Email: info@pekobooks.com · www.pekobooks.com

Author: Wilhelm Bender · Editing: Zsolt Darabos · Translating: Derik Hamond

Photos: Archive of Modern Conflict

Printed in Hungary · ISBN 978-615-5583-68-1

FOREWORD

On the 1 September 1939, on the border between Germany and Poland, the Second World War began. On 8 May 1945, the war in Europe ended with the unconditional surrender of the German Army. Almost no country was spared the monstrous juggernaut of a war which inflicted great misery, annihilation and devastation upon the people of the world.

Germany fought against Poland, Britain, Norway, Belgium, Luxemburg, Holland, France, Greece, Yugoslavia, Russia and the United States of America.

The nations allied to the Reich were Italy, Hungary, Romania, Bulgaria, Finland, Slovakia and Japan. However, apart from Hungary and Japan, these allies gradually fell away due to political upheavals in their own country.

This book should not be seen as a political document, nor does it discuss war crimes. My intention in this work is simply to focus on my war experiences.

September 1946
Wilhelm Bender

MILITARY CAREER OF WILHELM BENDER:

28 August 1939 - 4 March 1940
9./Infanterie-Regiment 485
5 March 1940 - 26 February 1942
3./San.Ersatz-Abteilung 12
27 February 1942 - 9 May 1943
Reserve Lazarett Lörchingen
10 May 1943 - 1 April 1944
3./leichte Artillerie-Abteilung 849 (RSO)
2 April 1944 - 24 August 1944
Stab/leichte Artillerie-Abteilung 849 (RSO)
25 August 1944 - 3 October 1944
5./leichte Artillerie-Abteilung 849 (RSO)
4 October 1944 - 11 February 1945
5./Heeres Festungs Artillerie-Abteilung 849
12 February 1945 - 8 May 1945
2./Heeres Artillerie-Abteilung 849

CHAPTER 1

SECURING THE GERMAN WESTERN BORDER IN THE SCHNEE-EIFEL REGION

(28 August 1939 – 4 March 1940)

On 28 August 1939, I was mobilized to the infantry and told to present myself to the Hutier Barracks in Darmstadt. Due to my training in the German Red Cross, I was posted as a medic to the 9. Komp. Inf. Regiment 485, which began its march to the western border of Germany after just a few days.

We were transferred to Schnee-Eifel on the German-Belgian border where we moved into the newly built Westwall (Siegfried Line), which was supposed to protect our homeland from invasion by the enemy. We were closest to the village of Hollerath in the Schleiden district. A beautiful, long autumn gave way to a very severe and cold winter which we spent in the bunkers of the Westwall and in a nearby Reichsarbeitsdienst (RAD) camp close to Reiferscheid until 17 December 1939. However, during this period, from 12 October until 37 October 1939, I was posted to Baasem in the Eifel district in order to take my military medical exams with the I.San.Komp.263.

Machine gun in position on the German-Belgian border.

A view of the Hökerlinie and the approaches to the German-Belgian border.

On the night of 18/19 December 1939, our regiment was transferred from the Western Front and taken by train to Bonn am Rhein. We remained for a few days in the neighbouring Beuel district where we also spent our first Christmas at war. Our battalion was assigned quarters in Uckerath, a beautiful and immaculately kept village. The severe coldness of 'Herr Winter' could not prevent us from carrying out various military exercises at both regimental and divisional level. Then, at the end of February 1940, a surprise order took us back to Bonn am Rhein, where we were housed in the city centre. I spent an intervening period of military leave, from 28 January 1940 to 10 February 1940, in the western part of my homeland.

* * *

The well-camouflaged bunkers that were our homes for a few weeks.
Both pictures show crew bunkers.

Exercises were always being held within the bunker line.

Our officers in their accommodation.

The Komp.Trupp of the 9.Komp. in the field.

Candidates taking part in the medical examination under the leadership of Oberarzt Dr. Roth from Mainz/Rh.

Our sickbay.

These pictures show the doctor and other ranks of the III. Bataillon in the courtyard of the hospital at Uckerath.

CHAPTER 2

WITH THE TROOPS OF OCCUPATION IN POLAND

(5 March 1940 – 17 August 1940)

In accordance with my wish to work directly in a medical unit I received a request, which was addressed to my division, to join the San.Ers.Abt.12 in Lodsch (Lodz) which was later renamed, briefly, Litzmannstadt. I travelled via Wehrkreisersatzdepot 12 (Military District Replacement Depot 12), located in Mainz, where I stayed for two days.

After a long and exhausting journey via Leipzig and Breslau my train arrived at the station in Lodsch shortly before midnight on the 9 March 1940. Deep snow lay on the streets of the sleeping town. Lodsch, after Warsaw, was the second largest city in Poland and had a population of around 700,000 of which 80% were Poles and Jews. They were not exactly pro-German, but they accepted the situation in which they now found themselves.

Because of my civilian occupation I was set to work as a Bekleidungs-Uffz. (clothing NCO) with the 3.Komp.. This new posting kept me very busy but I knew how to handle it. Day and night I dressed thousands of men who, a few days later, left our unit when they were posted to the frontline. This is how I spent the summer of 1940 in Poland. However, I was granted leave from 16 May 1940 until 31 May 1940 inclusive, which I spent in Ludwigshafen am Rhein, my hometown at that time.

* * *

Our kitchen staff in Lodsch.

The main street in Lodsch.

Our guard and 3.Komp. moving out in front of our accommodation in Lodsch – a former Jewish orphanage, which was empty.

In summer 1940 the German Wehrmacht in Lodsch were deployed to the east.

Together with comrades from the police we visited the air base.

Welcome donations from the homeland. ▲ ▶

CHAPTER 3

WITH THE SAN.ERS.ABT. 12 IN BAD KREUZNACH

(20 August 1940 - 26 February 1942)

After the campaign in France ended with a German victory, major shifts took place within the Wehrmacht. Troops from the east were relocated to the west and troops from the west were sent to the east while still others came to the Reich. San.Ers.Abt. 12 (medical staff replacement unit 12) also found itself involved in these moves and loaded in Lodsch on 18 August 1940 to travel to its new base in Bad Kreuznach.

In the early hours of 20 August 1940 we were enthusiastically received by the population and, to the sound of rousing music, moved into the Hindenburg Kaserne (Hindenburg Barracks). Fine weather accompanied us on the march through the town.

Bad Kreuznach, a beautiful old town in the renowned wine district of Nahetal (Nahe Valley), soon became familiar to those of us from the west of Germany. The locals, greatly pleased by the arrival of their new soldiers, went out of their way to contribute to the fine mutual understanding that developed between us and them.

After being promoted to San.Uffz. (NCO) on 1 September 1940, I was on the regular staff of the division and therefore had the prospect of remaining in Bad Kreuznach for a longer period of time. This meant I could bring my wife, who still lived in Ludwigshafen am Rhein, to Bad Kreuznach, where she remained until the end of the war. Luck had it that I was stationed with the same unit until February 1942 and was therefore able to spend many pleasant hours in the homeland area.

Until 15 December 1941, I was in charge of the 3.Komp. clothing store and was also the reserve clothing NCO for the entire division. I spent the last three months of my time in Bad Kreuznach with the staff, where I was assigned to special duties.

From 27 December 1941 until 15 February 1942, the German people contributed woollen and other articles of winter clothing for our troops on the Eastern Front. This large-scale collection campaign was organized and carried out by the offices of the municipalities and city administrations. As part of this campaign, I was seconded to the Wehrmacht's acceptance depot for the Bad Kreuznach and Bingerbrück districts.

A period of leave, from 13 to 28 July 1941, made the time I spent in beautiful Bad Kreuznach even more idyllic.

* * *

Marching into the Hindenburg Barracks to stirring music.

Staff surgeon Dr. Habermann, chief of 3.Komp.

Some of the buildings of the Hindenburg Barracks in Bad Kreuznach.

Under my direction the laundry was freshly prepared each week for issue to our comrades.

In front of my filing cabinet in the clothing store.

Our Spiess (sergeant major): Sepp Mühlfenzel.

Oberfeldarzt (chief doctor) Dr. Weissenbacher at the swearing in of new recruits.

Air-raid drill in Bad Kreuznach.

The whole company is put on alert.

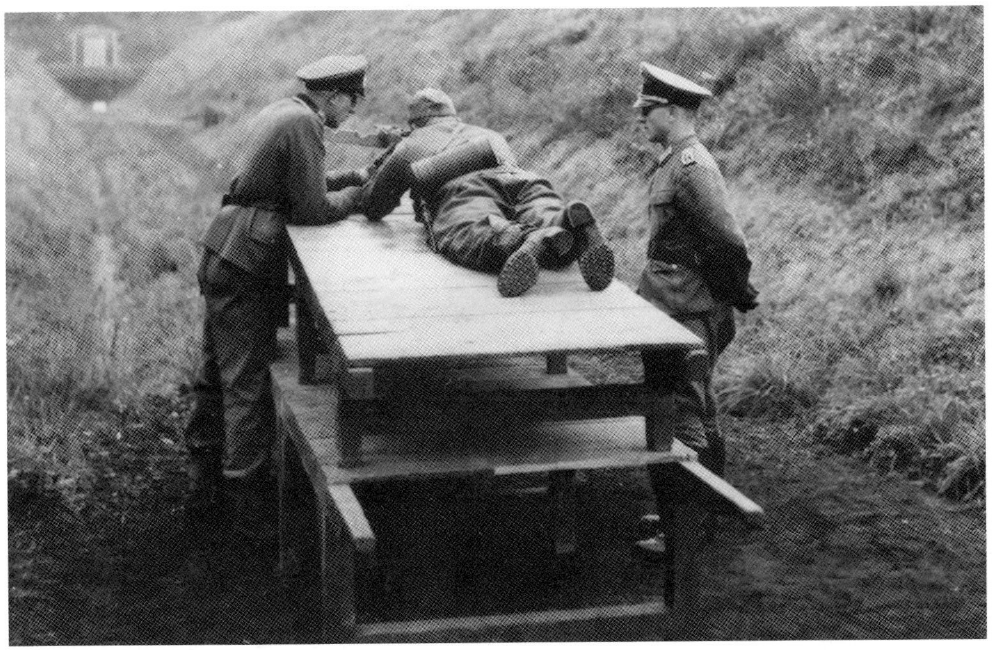

Caution. Live firing!

3.Komp. on the move.

Halt! Train approaching!

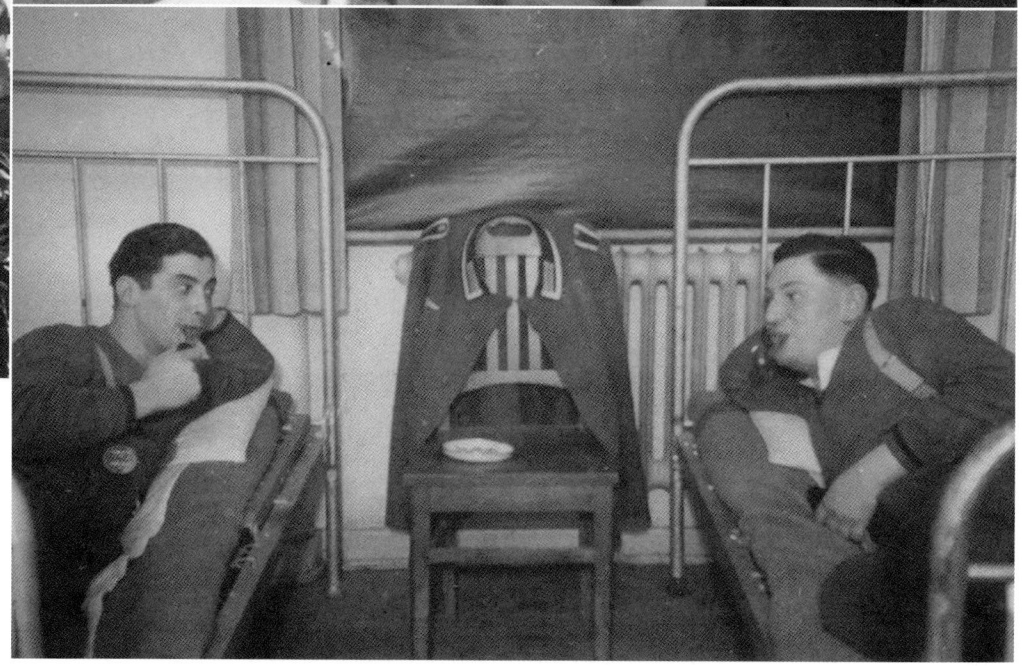

Room 65, the sergeants' mess in the Hindenburg Barracks in Bad Kreuznach.

CHAPTER 4

AT THE RESERVE FIELD HOSPITAL, LÖRCHINGEN

(27 February 1942 – 10 May 1943)

Finally, a long-awaited wish of mine was to come true; to get to know the workings of a field hospital better. With effect from 27 February 1942, I was transferred, via the San. Abteilung Metz, to the Heeres-Sanitätsstaffel (army medical battalion) in Lörchingen.

Here, under the effective leadership Oberstabsarzt (chief surgeon) Dr. Goebel, a reserve medical facility was established in a large psychiatric hospital and at the beginning of March 1942, he took control of the facility which, with its 350 beds, admitted wounded or sick soldiers serving on the fronts in the east, south and north. A conscientious staff, consisting of nurses from the German Red Cross and Sisters of Mercy from the Convent in Strassburg (Strasbourg), as well as selected army medical personnel, stood at the disposal of this military hospital.

Lörchingen (Lorquin) lay on the new German-French border or in other words, in formerly French territory. Its around 800 inhabitants consisted almost exclusively of French nationals but a satisfactory mutual understanding was established.

The location of Lörchingen, at the foot of the Vosges Mountains and on the rail line between Saarburg and Albersweiler, itself a branch of the main line to Paris, allowed the wounded and sick to spend a really pleasant time there.

For most of the medical staff too it must have been the most pleasant time of the war. Excellent officers, or rather doctors, led the hospital, so that there were never any disagreements. Camaraderie was always on display and as a consequence the organization of our spare time was never too difficult for us. We took smaller or longer walks on Sundays when off duty so that we got to know our local, and wider, environment. I frequently visited Saarbrücken and the old German town of Strassburg, where I would meet my wife. In this way I became familiar with the area which I grew to like immensely.

Twice I was lucky enough to go on vacation from Lörchingen: in May 1942 and over Christmas and New Year's Eve of the same year.

* * *

With my family, Christmas 1942.

The reserve hospital with its nursing and medical staff was established in Lörchingen at the beginning of February 1942 and then, at the beginning of the following March, placed under the leadership of Oberstabsarzt Dr. Goebel.

The doctors' quarters.

The nurses' quarters.

An old bunker in front of the hospital.

Uffz. Bender at the raising of the flag.

Our nurses from the Red Cross.

Nurses from the Sisters of the Convent.

On 13 March 1942 the first of the wounded arrived from the east.

French fuel depot at Lörchingen.

Tractors towing a ship in the canal.

A ship on the bridge.

Group of 'Sanis' by the canal bridge.

This is where we emptied many a jar, in beautiful Hermelingen (now Hermelange, France).

A short walk took us to the new border with France.

We often went for bicycle rides during off-duty hours.

Sergeant Bender with privates Toenges and Landmann going about their daily duties.

Michael Kundinger died in an accident on 5 June 1942.

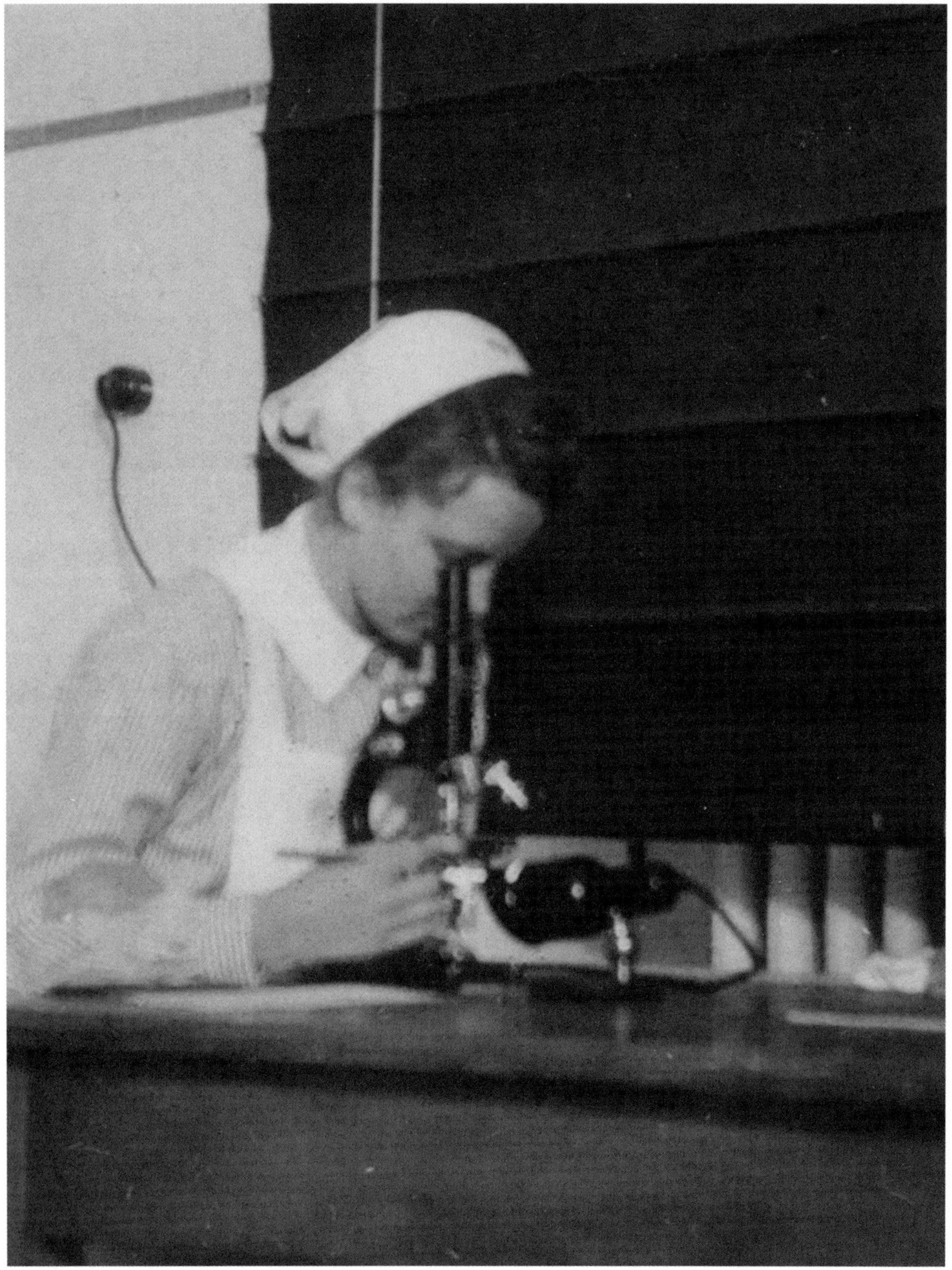
In the hospital's laboratory.

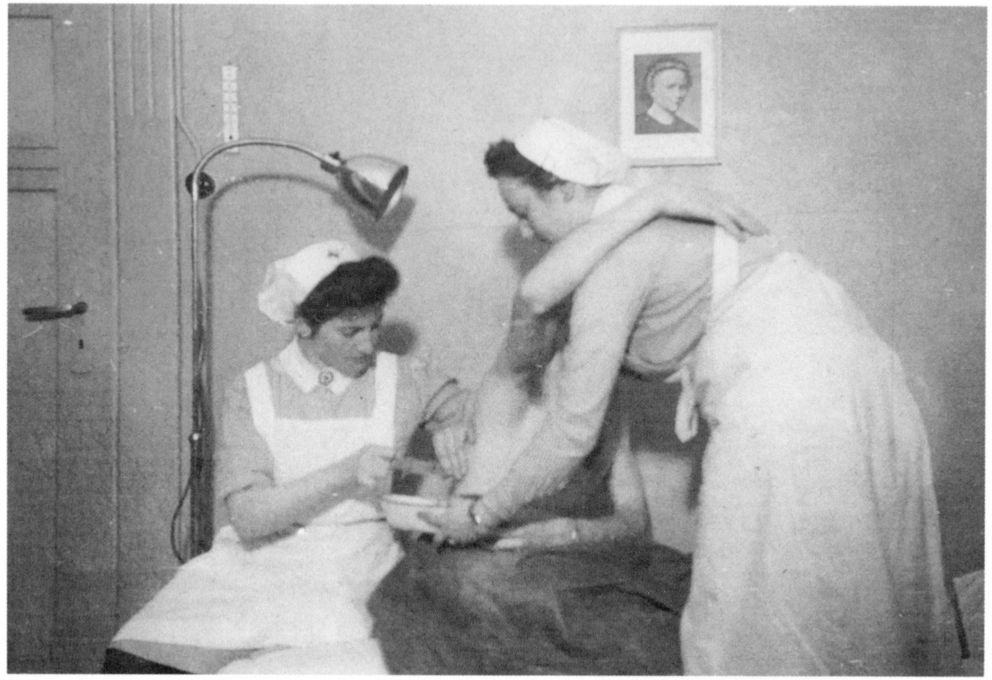
An injection is given.

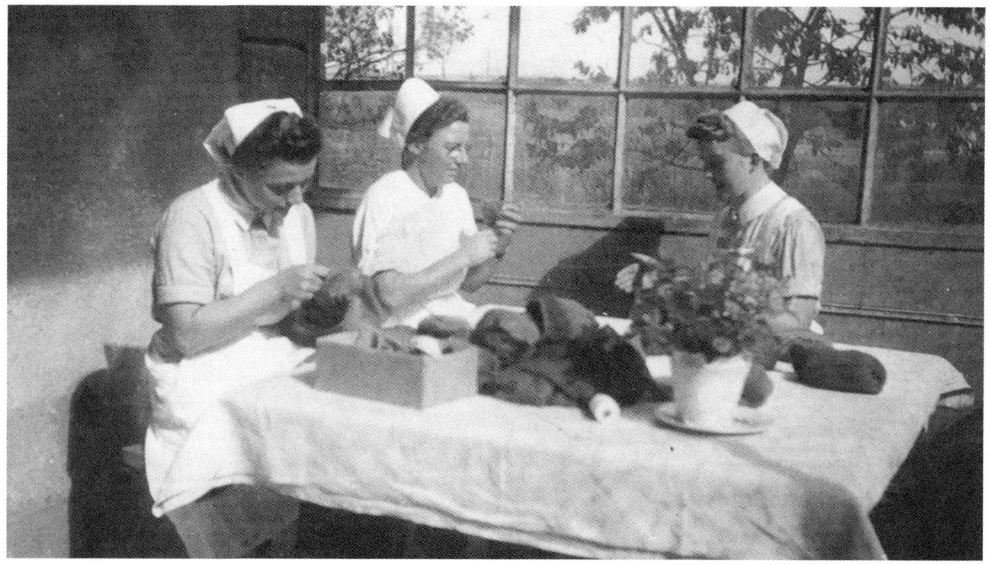
Nurses off duty.

Oberstabsarzt Dr. Goebel with Oberarzt Dr. Mann.

Oberarzt Dr. Mann in conversation with Sister Liselotte.

Personnel of Abt. 2.

Our Spiess (sergeant major) is in a good mood.

When Dr. Stoffel, our assistant surgeon, left the Lörchingen Reserve Hospital he was taken to the station by the entire personnel of our company. Dr. Stoffel was reassigned to the Eastern Front add to its strength. When an old comrade left the company he was always given a farewell escort.

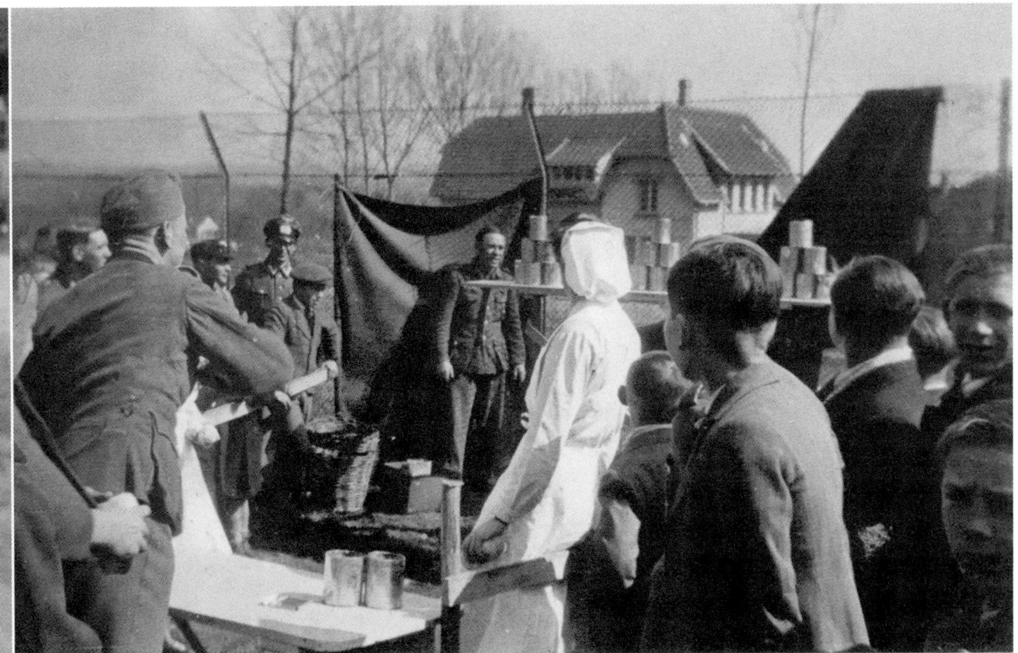

'Wehrmacht Day' was much celebrated in the Lörchingen Reserve Hospital. A great public festival, it was attended in substantial numbers by patients, company doctors, paramedics and nurses. The whole population was in good spirits.

On Sunday 19 July 1942, a few comrades from the Heer.San.Staffel Lörchingen made an interesting trip to the zone of the Maginot Line. We travelled by train via Saarburg and Finstingen to Saaralben, and from there marched via Holwingen and Remeringen to Püttlingen. Along the 15 km stretch of road, to the left and right of us, shot-up bunkers, wrecked dwellings and pulverised woodland told their own story of the pitiless combat that took place here. Püttlingen itself, where there was determined resistance, was reduced to 80 % rubble and ashes. The following pictures show the consequences of such a war.

* * *

Pictures of the ruins of Püttlingen an der Saar.

Saaralben too had suffered greatly in this war.

Saaralben after the destruction during the Westfeldzug (Western Campaign) 1940.

Things looked bad in Püttlingen too.

No stone stood atop another – that's war.

Immense emplacements on the Maginot Line.

The graves of German soldiers on the Maginot Line.

French tollhouse at Saarbrücken.

French anti-tank barriers between Saarbrücken und Forbach.

French bunker in German Strassburg.

CHAPTER 5

TRANSFER FROM SAN.ERS.ABT. 12 TO LE.ART.ABT. 849 (RSO)

(10 May 1943 – 13 July 1943)

In the war in the east, which had now lasted two years, Germany had already lost many of its best sons and urgent replacements were needed to make up these losses. An order from the OKH decreed that all those eligible, born as far back as 1910 and still within the home area, were to be transferred to the Eastern Front as rapidly as possible. Because France was now considered a 'home base', I too fell under this order and so, on 10 May 1943, I left my post at the Lörchingen Reserve Hospital, a posting that I had grown to love, to report for duty at San.Ers.- und Ausb.Abt. 12 (a medical personnel replacement and training unit) in Bad Kreuznach where I spent 10 days training in various skills.

On 21 May 1943, following an order issued by the Gen.Kdo. XII.A.K., I was transferred to le.Art.Abt. 849 (RSO) which was located in Baumholder for restructuring. I was assigned to the 3. Bttr. with the rank of medical orderly. The unit itself had managed to escape the Stalingrad encirclement and was now in the Reich for refitting and personnel replacement. Four light field howitzers, each with a calibre of 10.5cm, formed the heavy weaponry of each battery. For towing we were equipped with the newly released RSO (Raupenschlepper Ost).

Of course all this took a certain amount of time and so it was almost the middle of July by the time we were deployed. This made it possible for me to spend another beautiful summer's month in the homeland.

The medical orderlies of le.Art.Abt. 849 (RSO).

* * *

Leutnant Löwe and our Spiess, Hptw. Wolf, also appeared at the shooting range.

This is the Raupenschlepper.

Our new RSO towing vehicles arranged in ranks.

A closer look at our cannons.

And our trailers.

This picture shows two Wachtmeister (the artillery equivalent to the rank of Feldwebel/sergeant).

CHAPTER 6

DEFENSIVE COMBAT IN THE VICINITY OF OREL, BRJANSK

(14 July 1943 - 2 September 1943)

In the early hours of 14 July 1943 we said farewell to Baumholder, to our homeland and to Germany to travel onto our new deployment area in the distant east. Beautiful sunshine accompanied us on our five-day journey to that infamous land, Russia, the paradise of the Bolsheviks. We travelled via Berlin and eastern Germany, through Poland, past Warsaw, and crossed the Russian border at Brest-Litowsk. Onwards we travelled, via Minsk, Gomel, and Brjansk, to the area of Orel where the Russians had begun a large-scale offensive which was running in their favour.

We detrained and immediately travelled, without pause for breath, to our deployment area near Chistra where we experienced our baptism of fire on our first day. Here, difficult hours, or rather weeks, had to be endured during which some comrades from our unit sacrificed their lives. On some days the enemy's superior strength forced us to change position two or three times. The Red Army committed huge numbers of tanks and combat aircraft which in barely six weeks threw us to back to the area of Brjansk. All too often it was our unit that was deployed as the rearguard, a task which demanded the highest levels of performance of both personnel and materiel.

* * *

Le.Art.Abt. 849 (RSO) near Halle, on the way to the east. ▲ ▶

WH
1446996

Hauptmann Fink is the officer in charge of this massive column.

WH
1497 225

The field kitchen with its tempting pea soup is loaded too.

Toilets are provided during the transport operation.

Firing positions will be occupied.

Our vehicles are assembled.

Guns are brought into position.

The battery is set up.

Everything is in place.

The gunnery computation tent.

The first shells to the enemy.

This picture shows an observation position in thc combat zone around Orel.

On forward observer duty in the combat zone around Orel.

Firing position at Chistra.

Our chief, Hauptmann Fink, and our Spiess, Hauptw. Wolf, carrying out the duty of forward observer.

Our towing vehicles are well camouflaged from enemy planes.

Russian prisoners are brought in from the combat area around Orel.

They put themselves at the disposal of our troops, against their own folk.

Intense artillery activity around Orel.

San.Uffz. Bender gets the job of making sure we get fed.

Hauptmann Fink awards comrades the E.K. (Eiserne Kreuz/Iron Cross) and K.v.K. (Kriegsverdienstkreuz/War Merit Cross)

Russian planes heading towards us…the machine gun is made ready.

Inside one of our many firing positions.

Hauptmann Fink driving his Volkswagen on the lookout for a new position.

A well-camouflaged gun.

The vehicles get started again.

A break in the combat.

CHAPTER 7

DEFENSIVE COMBAT AROUND BRJANSK, ON THE DNIEPER AND THE RETREAT TO THE SSOSCH

(3 September 1943 – 27 December 1943)

The unrelenting pressure of the enemy forced us to concede significant territory. Changes of position, one after the other and sometimes by as much as 100 km a day, had to be made in order to avoid the enemy's pincer movements. Nevertheless, the Red Army managed to encircle us on the Desna (a tributary of the Dnieper River) for four days.

Heavy fighting broke out during which our battery chief, Hauptmann Fink, died a hero's death. We were already imagining ourselves marching into Russian captivity when, in the nick of time, the 5. Panzer-Division was deployed to open up a gap in the encirclement. This allowed us to escape the encirclement albeit under great duress. We withdrew further and crossed the Dnieper at Brjansk. We passed by Potschep and continued our retreat towards the River Ssosch. Only at this location did our troops succeed in bringing the frontline to a standstill for a few weeks.

Our unit was deployed along the line of the Ssosch River where the construction of a small defensive position was immediately begun. Leutnant Löwe who, since the heroic death of Hauptmann Fink, had been acting as our battery chief handed over its command to a new chief, Oberleutnant Dr. Heinrich Steitz.

In mid-November the enemy lauched a new attack which, with its numerous tanks and aircraft, forced us after heavy and eventful combat into renewed withdrawal manoeuvres. Gomel and the Shlobin bridgehead were abandoned and the front could only once again be brought to a standstill at Iskra.

This made it possible to experience Germany's most beautiful festival, Christmas, in relative peace. We spent the festive period in old straw huts which were occasionally destroyed by the impact of enemy shells. Unfortunately, a few of our comrades were unable to spend Christmas 1943 with us; a soldier's death or wounds had torn them from our midst. But, in spirit, they were still there to share with us those difficult hours of winter of 1943/44.

For me, this difficult and sombre period on the Eastern Front was shortened by a period of leave, from 23 October 1943 until 15 November 1943, which I spent in Bad Kreuznach.

* * *

The unit undertakes a major change in position for a new mission.

Vehicle after vehicle on the dusty tracks of the central section of the Eastern Front.

A pause in a village for refuelling and so on.

A short break inside the Russian encirclement.

What will happen to us?

We crossed the Desna after heavy fighting and managed to escape encirclement by the Russians.

Firing positions on the Desna.

An Iron Cross is awarded.

We see nothing but burning villages during our retreat.

Taking cover in an anti-tank ditch.

Wachtmeister Kleinlagel in the field.

Oberleutnant Schneider, Leutnant Löwe and Ass. Arzt Dr. Behrendt near Wettka.

The new battery chief, Dr. Heinrich Steits, arrives in a Volkswagen.

Dr. Heinrich Steits, Oberleutnant and chief of the battery, at the command post.

Out unit had an outpost in Babin.

The enemy is behind us.

This is my bunker.

Brisk enemy activity forces us to construct bunkers immediately.

A few days later these was yet another change of position in the bridgehead but still within the Shlobin sector.

Snow covers the firing position.

In a foxhole.

A view of our firing position in the Shlobin bridgehead.

A break in the firing.

Changing position.

On the Russian supply tracks.

Soldiers' graveyard in the east.

Greetings from Iskra.

Our command post in Iskra.

Firing position in Iskra.

This is where our gunnery coordination post was located.

CHAPTER 8

DEFENSIVE COMBAT AROUND PRIPJET AND WHITE RUSSIA

(28 December 1943 – 1 April 1944)

In the final days of December fighting again broke out on both sides which meant that we had to carry out major positional changes which brought us to the familiar area of Pripjet.

Deep snow alternating with deep mud covered the barely passable tracks on which our RSOs moved masterfully. Not a day went by in which our guns did not give everything they possibly could but the enemy nevertheless succeeded forcing us during these winter battles into further retreats.

Our withdrawal continued step by step until we finally reached White Russia (Belarus). It was only here that the enemy's strong pressure slackened somewhat the frontline became more stable.

In this sector, which was sometimes very lively, there were however a few days without much combat which allowed us briefly to live like humans. Again the familiar order to construct bunkers came into effect. However, it must be stated that building bunkers on the Eastern Front was for many soldiers a means of saving their lives.

* * *

A glimpse inside a firing position in the Pripjet sector.

Washing still has to be done.

And potatoes have to be peeled.

Building bunkers at the firing position in the mud of Pripjet.

More military decorations are issued.

Oberleutnant Steits and Wachtmeister Kleinlagel doing their rounds.

Major Werner, our commander, in our position.

A Volkswagen drives in deep snow on a Russian road.

Our firing positions in the deep snow of the central sector of the frontline.

Salvo after salvo hits the enemy!

The battery chief on his way to inspect the vehicles.

These empty shell crates show what our battery fired in one day.

Our RSOs demanded particular care and attention on the Eastern Front.

Supplies continually need to be replenished. ▲ ▶

A glimpse into a firing position located within a birch forest.

The battery's radio post was located in this bunker.

The chief, the battery officers and others make their daily inspection tour.

Wachtmeister Heinrich Kleinlagel always accompanies the tour.

Battery Chief Oberleutnant Steits with the guns.

The guns were always ready for action.

Leutnant Löwe also makes his inspection tour.

Weapon inspections were also frequently carried out on the Eastern Front.

Leutnant Löwe himself was there.

CHAPTER 9

THE BATTLE OF KOWEL

(2 April 1944 – 4 May 1944)

In response to a sudden order our unit loaded onto two trains for transport via Minsk, Baranowitsche, Bret-Litowsk, Lublin and Colm to the combat sector around Kowel.

The enemy had suddenly succeeded in encircling the Kowel in which many military as well as civilian administrative offices were located. Our mission was to liberate the town. A large number of tanks, combat aircraft and artillery pieces were assembled in the area to provide the infantry with secure support.

On 6 April 1944 our troops, after heavy fighting, managed to force their way into Kowel and threw back the enemy who had surrounded it for 16 days. Our unit, which played an active role in the relief of the town, then took part in subsequent battles while attached to Heeresgruppe Mitte (Army Group Centre).

From 15 April, I was assigned to the staff of our unit where I, together Dr. Behrendt and San. Oberfeldwebel Tanz, helped set up a first aid station.

Kowel itself had suffered greatly during the recent fighting and was also subsequently, and understandably, the target of enemy aircraft and artillery. Unfortunately our unit suffered very heavy casualties in Kowel and we had to lay some of our comrades to rest there.

Following the liberation of Kowel our unit commander, Hauptmann Werner, was promoted to Major and Hauptmann Wagner (2. Batterie) and Oberleutnant Steits (3. Batterie) were awarded the Deutsches Kreuz (German Cross) in Gold.

* * *

We were in the central section of the frontline when we were suddenly loaded onto trains to be taken to a 'hotspot' in the southern sector of the Eastern Front; the combat sector of Kowel.

Fe.Wg.

A firing emplacement in the vicinity of Kowel. Vehicles are dug in. ▲ ▶

Foxholes are important.

Here come the enemy planes.

Panzerzug (armoured train) 72 was also deployed in the Kowel sector.

Unt 18.12.42
Br Unt 23.11.43 Bsl

German armour on the move in the vicinity of Kowel.

Kamerad Baumann at work.

Oberleutnant Steits and Leutnant Heitmann.

Lots of heavy weapons were deployed.

After the liberation of Kowel by German troops, both German and Russian tanks could frequently be seen in the streets; some of them burnt out or otherwise rendered useless for combat.

After the liberation of Kowel.

Kowel itself had suffered greatly, as these pictures show.

This was the H.V.Pl. (Hauptverbandplatz) in Kowel.

The T.V.Pl. (Truppenverbandplatz) in Kowel.

The supply base in battle-sector Kowel.

Gunnery coordination base and kitchen vehicles in the vicinity of Kowel.

CHAPTER 10

POSITIONAL BATTLES WITH THE 12. KÖNIGL. HONVÉD-DIVISION IN THE SECTOR OF HEERESGRUPPE NORD-UKRAINE

(5 May 1944 – 13 July 1944)

The fighting in and around Kowel was over and our mission there fulfilled. However, a new order decreed another entrainment that took us to Malorita in northern Ukraine. From here, our detachment marched overland to new positions about 15km behind Gorniki. This sector of the frontline, which was still completely quiet, was controlled and occupied by the 12. Königl. Ung. Honvéd-Reserve-Division to which our unit was subordinated.

After the hard weeks we had just been through, we found this new position thoroughly relaxing. The weather too was on our side so that we gradually began to feel human again.

Cooperating with our Hungarian comrades was very satisfying, a situation which repeatedly found expression in our joint operations.

I was not to witness the last three weeks spent by our unit in this posting because, on the very day on which a general ban on leave was announced, I was able to travel to Bad Mergentheim to spend my last annual leave with my wife and sister.

* * *

Our transport train on the way to Malorita in northern Ukraine. ▲ ▶

LüP 11.50 m
Ladegew.
Tragf.
Bodenfl.
Ladelänge
15000 kg
17500 kg
27 m²
10.1 m
Stuttgart
23058
Stuttgart
23058

Darkness falls as soon as we have unloaded.

Arrival in Malorita.

In front of a Hungarian Hauptverbandplatz in northern Ukraine.

A Hungarian soldiers' graveyard close to the Hauptverbandplatz in Ukraine.

Hungarian infantrymen advance to the forwardmost line.

Abteilung 849's first aid tent in a wood in northern Ukraine.

Planning a crackdown on partisans.

CHAPTER 11

DISENGAGEMENT MANOEUVRES ON THE EASTERN FRONT; FROM THE BUG TO THE WEICHSEL

(14 July 1944 – 24 August 1944)

Suddenly, and unexpectedly, at the beginning of July 1944 the Russians began a large-scale summer offensive. This pushed back our frontline and almost caused its complete collapse. With unprecedented speed the Red Army's armoured spearheads smashed through our lines and in a few weeks succeeded in throwing back our troops over the River Bug and as far as the Weichsel (Vistula).

Some divisions were annihilated or taken prisoner. Miraculously most of our division escaped although we were caught in the middle of this great struggle. We withdrew via Wlodawa, Hanna and Sielche to Warsaw. Almost all of our guns and vehicles fell into enemy hands or were blown up. As far as Sielche the enemy matched our pace and was sometimes only 20 metres away although they never succeeded in encircling us which they were determined to do whatever the circumstances. In Warsaw we gathered the remains of our Abteilung. We remained on the grounds of the airfield and after three days marched to Lowitsch where we set up an assembly area for our unit.

Here we were able to take the rest we needed so desperately. Our retreat had been more or less a race against death that demanded nerves of steel. At last, in this land of Poland, blessed by God, we could spend hours of reflection and recuperation.

* * *

The Abteilung is more or less a coherent unit during the retreat. ▲ ▶

Heading westwards.

In Polish territory. ▲ ▶

A short mid-day break for lunch is taken.

The whole of the central sector is on the move.

The roads leading westwards are always packed.

The difficult hours around Sielche are behind us. ▼ ▶

A short break is taken at Wlodawa where we cross the River Bug.

Onwards to Warsaw.

The remains of our Abteilung roll through Warsaw, Poland.

We assembled on the airfield in Warsaw. ▲ ▶

The mood has improved; the enemy did not get us. ▲ ▶

On the grounds of Warsaw Airport. ▲ ▶

The Volkswagen, our trusted companion.

The headquarters was based here for a few days.

CHAPTER 12

REFITTING IN EAST PRUSSIA AND SUBORDINATION TO HEERES FEST. ART. ABT. 849

(25 August 1944 – 12 September 1944)

Our unit, which was badly damaged by the retreat along the entire Eastern Front, was supposed to be reformed in the district of Soldau in East Prussia. For this purpose it travelled partly by road and partly by train to Grallau, where the staff was quartered.

After just a few days there, our unit was reorganized into five batteries. The 5. Batterie, to which I was assigned in the meantime, moved into quarters in Niostoj, a small and immaculate village in the Soldau district.

We spent almost 14 peaceful days here and then, after a successful farewell evening with the locals, we travelled to the fortress at Modlin where we were equipped as a Heeres Festungs-Artillerie-Abteilung. Each of our five batteries received four 12.2cm guns and three 7.5cm guns, that is to say our Abteilung received a total of 35 new tubes. These guns had all been captured from the Russians.

In the fortress itself, in order to prepare us for our forthcoming tasks, we received training on how to use our new guns. After a few days we were sent to Neu Modlin, a small village behind Modlin itself, where we could again relax in peace.

* * *

We leave our old assembly area in Lowitsch. ▼ ▶

A short rest during a break in travelling.

Good spirits all round because the refitting will take place in the Reich. ▼ ▶

We spent the night here.

The NCOs of the new 5. Batterie in Niostoj.

The '849' at the station in Niostoj.

Arriving In Modlin.

Oberwachtmeister Glaunsinger keeps watch.

Everyone helps unload the munitions from the wagons.

The train is empty…now we move on.

Inside Festung Modlin.

View from the fortress tower.

Firing emplacement in Neu Modlin.

Training on the guns.

Our new guns.

Russian 12.2cm gun.

CHAPTER 13

SUPPRESSION OF THE POLISH UPRISING IN WARSAW

(13 September – 3 October 1944)

In the capital city of Poland, Warsaw, a large-scale armed uprising by the Polish Home Army began on 1 August 1944.

Behind the German front line, which was constantly being driven back, this threatened to develop into a dangerous situation that had to be countered by every means possible. The insurgents, which consisted of two groups (nationalists and the communists) suddenly occupied official buildings such as post offices and railways and soon controlled the streets. The Russians, who had pledged their support for the Poles, had in the meantime pushed into the district of Praga on the opposite bank of the River Weichsel.

In recognition of the threat posed, on the night of 13 September 1944 the OKH ordered our Abteilung to move to Warsaw with our all of our 35 guns in order to take an active role in suppressing the uprising.

Through rubble and ashes, we drove through streets lined by charred masonry into a city in flames. Warsaw was in ruins.

We took up firing positions on the southern edge of the city. Our 4. Batterie under Oberleutnant Löwe, was located in a large horticultural establishment. As soon as we had our guns set up and had reported them ready for action, a hail of heavy calibre shells began to rain down on our position. We had clearly been betrayed because our position had been precisely identified and targeted.

Nevertheless, we remained in this position for almost three whole days because our deployment from this location was required to support our brave infantry who were involved in bitter house-to-house combat in the centre of the city. Our shells were supposed to disrupt the activity of the enemy on the opposite side of the Weichsel.

On 16 September 1944 we at last moved to a new firing position right next to Warsaw West Station and from there rejoined the raging battle with renewed vigour.

The Polish Home Army was immensely strong and the rebels put up tremendous resistance against our troops but eventually, after particularly fierce house-to-house fighting, the rebels surrendered the city piece by piece. On 3 October 1944, when the bloody uprising in Warsaw came to an end, 27,000 women and men of the Polish Home Army marched into German captivity. Following this, the combat against the Russians over the Weichsel continued with undiminished intensity.

To conclude this brief description of the Warsaw Uprising, it must be stated that it was probably one of the bloodiest episodes of the war and one that only had such a fatal beginning due to shortsightedness. No battlefield in this epic war could have claimed so many victims in such a short time as was the case in Warsaw. It must be reiterated here too that the beautiful capital of Poland was left completely reduced to ash and rubble.

* * *

A view of our first firing position in Warsaw during the Warsaw Uprising.

This is where the command post and gunnery coordination tent were set up.

The radio post and first aid facility had been set up in this glass house.

In a state of permanent readiness.

Our officers in front of the glass house.

CHAPTER 14

SECURING FORTRESS WARSAW

(4 October 1944 – 16 January 1945)

Warsaw was designated as a fortress when the uprising by the Polish Home Army was over. Infantry and combat engineers as well as our own Abteilung were deployed to secure the city.

And so it was that we remained in our positions which from now on were strengthened to form a stronghold. Accommodation bunkers and gun emplacements were constructed as well as various alternative firing positions to provide all-round protection. The Polish civilian population was commandeered to upgrade our positions and this went smoothly under our supervision.

The Russians, who were on the other bank of the Weichsel, generally conducted themselves very calmly so that, for us, a rather nice time began.

By order of the chief doctor of the IX. Armee Korps I was promoted to Sanitäts Feldwebel (medical orderly sergeant) with effect from 1 November 1944. We were able to mark this promotion with a small ceremony held under the circumstances prevailing at that time.

We were also able to spend Christmas and New Year's Eve in Fortress Warsaw until an enemy attack was launched at the beginning of January.

* * *

Our chief, Oberleutnant Löwe.

Behind our firing position.

There are accommodation bunkers here too.

Gun emplacements were constructed and blended into the terrain.

The barrel rears up from the gun emplacement.

Our anti-tank gun emplacement.

Lunch arrives.

The 'grunts' slowly make their way to the feeding points…for pea soup.

In front of the signals squad's accommodation in Warsaw.

Staff doctor, Dr. med. Wolter.

Motorcycle courier Obergefreiter Drescher.

Polish civilians.

Polish civilians at their daily work…building positions for us.

CHAPTER 15

DISENGAGEMENT MANOEUVRES BY HEERESGRUPPE WEICHSEL (17 January 1945 – 11 February 1945)

In the first days of January, a grim coldness and a period of heavy, new snowfall began but even during this harsh weather it was warm and snug in our bunker.

Suddenly, on 13 January 1945, the enemy lauched a new winter offensive in the Warka bridgehead. In our section of the frontline it was still dead quiet although we had to be prepared for anything. However, during the coming three days the Red Army came to within a few kilometres of encircling Warsaw from Warka und Modlin.

We were just about to move into our fortress position in the centre of Warsaw on the night of 16-17 January when the commandant of city, Generalleutnant Weber, simultaneously ordered the immediate demolition of our guns and the evacuation of the city. With far-sightedness, and after consideration of the situation in which we now found ourselves, Generalleutnant Weber and our Abteilung commander, Major Werner, who was also the fortress artillery commander, gave this clear order which enabled countless people to escape certain death. For this, these gentlemen were later brought before a court martial.

This order was executed rapidly and with the highest priority because only a few hours separated us from annihilation. To save our skins we left the town at a brisk pace. Partly on foot, partly aboard trucks we set off in wild haste, chased by the tanks and aircraft of the Red Army.

Having only just escaped an encirclement we soon found ourselves in another one. In a single night, together with some comrades from my unit, I took part in three successful breakouts. After a few days we arrived in Greudenz, stragglers dressed only in tattered clothes. We travelled onwards via Schweetz, across Tucheler-Heide (which was crawling with partisans) and onto Konitz where the few of us that were left formed a strongpoint in Sternau, about 12 km east of Konitz.

This chaos and confusion had scattered our whole Abteilung to the winds, and unfortunately quite a few comrades were taken prisoner, were wounded, or died a hero's death.

The Russians meanwhile pushed further west along the whole frontline with the aim of bringing down our capital, Berlin, which they later succeeded in doing. At the same time, British and American troops in the west pushed further into the interior of the Reich so that the prospect of a German final victory had disappeared. Our leadership however, which had become tyrannical, failed to recognized this fact and forced us to continue the absolutely pointless fighting.

* * *

CHAPTER 16

REFITTING AS HEERES ART. ABT. 849 IN POMERANIA (12 February 1945 – 8 March 1945)

On 12 February 1945, by order of the army, our Abteilung, which had been badly mauled during the withdrawal from Warsaw, was relocated to Pomerania for further reorganization.

We came to the district of Bütow, where only two batteries were set up from our previous four batteries. In Klein Tuchen and then in Schimmerwitz we spent a few days without having to fight. Leutnant Labs was in charge of the new 2. Batterie to which I had been assigned. We also received new traction vehicles very quickly, almost all of them new 'Mulis' (Sd.Kfz. 3, otherwise known as the Mautltier) . Then we waited for our guns. In the meantime the enemy had managed to reach the Baltic Sea near Colmar, so that we were again in a cauldron, which was, however, still quite large. But the operations of the Red Army went so smoothly that after just a few days our assembly area came under threat. So, without having received any artillery, we left Schimmerwitz in the early morning hours of 8 March to drive towards the Baltic Sea. A few hours later the Russians moved into our abandoned quarters.

Terrible scenes met our eyes; a vast number of refugees who had so desperately tried to escape the enemy lay on the streets. The lot of these poor people was made worse by the grim and persistent coldness to which many children and women in particular fell victim.

* * *

CHAPTER 17

DEFENSIVE BATTLES IN THE DANZIG BRIDGEHEAD AND WEICHSEL VALLEY (9 March 1945 – 14 April 1945)

After travelling through Neustadt, Gotenhafen and Sopot we reached the beautiful old city of Danzig which had also become part of the frontline. There was still lively activity in the streets of the city but it fell into the hands of the enemy a few days later.

Since no guns had yet arrived for our Abteilung it was deployed as an observation unit in the bridgehead. However, because our Abteilung lost 150 wounded and dead in the first three days of its new mission, I remained in Danzig to set up a first aid facility in the Langfuhr district.

Bombs fell down continuously on Danzig and enemy artillery fire pounded the centre of the city. The losses among the population and the troops stationed there were immense. It hardly needs to be said that, day and night, I had my hands full because, apart from a female hospital assistant, I stood alone, without a doctor or other help.

On 24 March 1945 Danzig, now completely destroyed, fell into Russian hands. A few hours earlier we received artillery pieces and were once more deployed as artillerymen.

Our new mission was in the Weichsel lowlands. As the area under our control continued to shrink, the hardships we suffered in the Heubude Forest, which was literally torn to shreds by enemy planes, grew ever more difficult to bear.

* * *

CHAPTER 18

ON THE FRISCHE NEHRUNG

(15 April 1945 – 8 May 1945)

Driven more and more into a corner by the enemy, we moved via Steegen and Stutthof to the Frische Nehrung, a narrow peninsular spit of land about 800 to 1000 metres wide and approximately 70 kilometres long. With the Baltic Sea on one side and a freshwater lagoon called the Frisches Haff on the other, this peninsula stretches towards the northeast.

Pillau, a town lying on the north side of the channel connecting the Frisches Haff and the Baltic Sea, fell into Russian hands and the enemy also succeeded in landing at a point 6 kilometres from the tip of the Frische Nehrung. Our fate on the peninsula was thus sealed; we were surrounded by water. Slowly, after heavy losses on both sides, kilometre by kilometre was given up in order to bring our troops to safety by ship. Our Abteilung did not share in this good fortune because, as an artillery unit, we were required to provide constant cover for the withdrawal of other units to the transport ships.

The strong pressure of the enemy increased, especially on 7 and 8 May 1945. Wave after wave of Russian attack aircraft incessantly dropped bombs on our positions. As a result of these attacks the enemy succeeded in destroying all the guns and vehicles of the 2. Batterie at a position 56 kilometres from the tip of the peninsula.

We were still shocked by this serious blow when, during the night of 8 May, news of the unconditional surrender of the German forces reached us. Our Abteilung assembled in the woods around Steegen and from there marched in columns into Russian captivity.

I would like to note too that I suffered my only wound on the Frische Nehrung. On 29 April 1945, I received a small wound on the little finger of my left hand when it was hit by a splinter from an exploding bomb.

* * *

CHAPTER 19

CAPITULATION

After the Anglo-American troops had advanced as far as the Elbe River, French troops occupied the Black Forest and Berlin fell into the hands of the Russians in the first days of May. This completed the occupation of Germany. Hitler's military successor, Admiral Dönitz, was forced to declare the unconditional surrender of the German forces to the three victorious powers; Great Britain, the United States of America and the Soviet Union, as well as to the French Republic.

The declaration was signed in Flensburg and this was subsequently announced to the world. On 8 May 1945 at 23.00 hours, a general truce came into effect on all fronts.

With this, the greatest war of all time, The Second World War, came to an end.

* * *

Wilhelm Bender